Journal Of Faith With Abba

And without faith it is impossible to please God, because anyone who comes to him must believe that he exists and that he rewards those who earnestly seek him.

Hebrews 11:6

Apostle Kendra

HerLife HerWrite Publishing Co. LLC

ISBN: 978-1-7373740-0-8

Dedication

This 90 day journal is dedicated to my precious Elohim above. He has directed and guided my path when I was in the World, loved me unconditionally, and protected me every step of the way. Now looking back on my journey up until now, I see why things occurred in my life and what was brought out of me to embark upon the calling that is on my life. I am now on a journey of glory, His glory, and I give it all back to Him. The journey that I am embarking upon with Yahweh is now stepping into Romans 8:18 & Peter 5:10.

This journal is for women and men of Elohim to reflect and totally embark upon the awesome journey Abba has for you! This journal will give you a more intimate relationship with Elohim and get your prophetic flow going. This is so Yahweh can open you up for a complete manifestation in him. Giving you clarity, revelation, and to help pull the ministry and business ideas out of you.

This journal is also for you to dive deeper into scripture, the reason for this journal being scripture based. You should reflect on what the scripture gives you spiritually as you read them, but also want to read the bible more for evaluation, wisdom, knowledge, and the instruction of Elohim, through Yahweh.

Welcome
to your First 7 Days
on your Faith Journey
with ABBA

Reflect on the scriptures.
Write down what comes to your mind and
spirit. Express where the verse takes you
spiritually.

Tracking Faith with Abba

Keep track of your journey as you go.

Day 1	
Day 2	
Day 3	
Day 4	
Day 5	
Day 6	
Day 7	

Day 1) Psalms 119:105

Your Word is a lamp for my feet, a light on my path.

Day 2) James 1:2-5

Consider it pure joy, my brothers and sisters, whenever you face trials of many kinds, because you know that the testing of your faith produces perseverance. Let perseverance finish its work so that you may be mature and complete, not lacking anything. If any of you lacks wisdom, you should ask God, who gives generously to all without finding fault, and it will be given to you.

Day 3) Galatians 5:22

But the fruit of the Spirit is love, joy, peace, forbearance, kindness, goodness, faithfulness,

Day 4) Hebrews 11:1

Now faith is confidence in what we hope for and assurance about what we do not see.

Day 5) Genesis 1:26-27

Then God said, "Let us make mankind in our image, in our likeness, so that they may rule over the fish in the sea and the birds in the sky, over the livestock and all the wild animals, and over all the creatures that move along the ground." So God created mankind in his own image, in the image of God he created them; male and female he created them.

Day 6) Proverbs 16:9

In their hearts humans plan their course, but the Lord establishes their steps

Day 7) 2 Thessalonians 3:3

But the Lord is faithful, and he will strengthen you and protect you from the evil one.

Next 7 Days
on Your Faith
Journey with ABBA

Get in your reflection mode.
Write down key phrases or words that come to
mind and spirit. Express where the verse takes
you spiritually.

Tracking Faith with Abba

Keep track of your journey as you go.

Day 1	
Day 2	
Day 3	
Day 4	
Day 5	
Day 6	
Day 7	

Day 8) Psalms 91:11

For he will command his angels concerning you to guard you in all your ways

Day 9) Jeremiah 33:3

Call to me and I will answer you and tell you great and unsearchable things you do not know.

Day 10) 1st Peter 2:9

But you are a chosen people, a royal priesthood, a holy nation, God's special possession, that you may declare the praises of him who called you out of darkness into his wonderful light.

Day 11) Matthew 6:33

But seek first his kingdom and his righteousness, and all these things will be given to you as well.

Day 12) 1st Peter 5:7

Cast all your anxiety on him because he cares for you

Day 13) Deuteronomy 31:8

The Lord himself goes before you and will be with you; he will never leave you nor forsake you. Do not be afraid; do not be discouraged.

Day 14) Mark 11:22-24

"Have faith in God," Jesus answered."Truly, I tell you, if anyone says to this mountain, 'Go, throw yourself into the sea,' and does not doubt in their heart but believes that what they say will happen, it will be done for them. Therefore I tell you, whatever you ask for in prayer, believe that you have received it, and it will be yours.

Next 7 Days
on Your Faith
Journey with ABBA

For these 7 days reflect. More so, write what you are hearing only in the scripture and where the verse takes you spiritually.

Tracking Faith with Abba

Keep track of your journey as you go.

Day 1	
Day 2	
Day 3	
Day 4	
Day 5	
Day 6	
Day 7	

Day 15) Proverbs 3:5-6

Trust in the Lord with all your heart
and lean not on your own understanding;
in all your ways submit to him,
and he will make your paths straight.

Day 16) Romans 12:2

Do not conform to the pattern of this world but be transformed by
the renewing of your mind. Then you will be able to test and
approve what God's will is—his good, pleasing and perfect will

Day 17) Luke 21:15

For I will give you words and wisdom that none of your adversaries will be able to resist or contradict

Day 18) Psalms 37:7-9

Be still before the Lord and wait patiently for him;
do not fret when people succeed in their ways,
when they carry out their wicked schemes.
Refrain from anger and turn from wrath;
do not fret—it leads only to evil.
For those who are evil will be destroyed,
but those who hope in the Lord will inherit the land

Day 19) Isaiah 43:2

When you pass through the waters,
    I will be with you;
and when you pass through the rivers,
    they will not sweep over you.
When you walk through the fire,
    you will not be burned;
    the flames will not set you ablaze

Day 20) Nehemiah 8:10

Nehemiah said, "Go and enjoy choice food and sweet drinks, and send some to those who have nothing prepared. This day is holy to our Lord. Do not grieve, for the joy of the Lord is your strength."

Day 21) Exodus 14:14

The Lord will fight for you; you need only to be still."

Next 7 Days
on your Faith Journey
with Abba

These next 7 days reflect and write what you are seeing. Write where the verse takes you spiritually.

Tracking Faith with Abba

Keep track of your journey as you go.

Day 1	
Day 2	
Day 3	
Day 4	
Day 5	
Day 6	
Day 7	

Day 22) Jeremiah 17:7-8

But blessed is the one who trusts in the Lord,
whose confidence is in him.
They will be like a tree planted by the water
that sends out it roots by the stream.
It does not fear when heat comes;
its leaves are always green.
It has no worries in a year of drought
and never fails to bear fruit."

Day 23) Isaiah 41:10

So do not fear, for I am with you;
     do not be dismayed, for I am your God.
I will strengthen you and help you;
     I will uphold you with my righteous right hand.

Day 24) Romans 15:13

May the God of hope fill you with all joy and peace as you trust in him, so that you may overflow with hope by the power of the Holy Spirit.

Day 25) Ephesians 6:10-12

Finally, be strong in the Lord and in his mighty power. Put on the full armor of God, so that you can take your stand against the devil's schemes. For our struggle is not against flesh and blood, but against the rulers, against the authorities, against the powers of this dark world and against the spiritual forces of evil in the heavenly realms.

Day 26) 1 Chronicles 16:11

Look to the Lord and his strength; seek his face always

Day 27) Mark 12:30

Love the Lord your God with all your heart and with all your soul and with all your mind and with all your strength.

Day 28) Matthew 6:25-27

"Therefore I tell you, do not worry about your life, what you will eat or drink; or about your body, what you will wear. Is not life more than food, and the body more than clothes? Look at the birds of the air; they do not sow or reap or store away in barns, and yet your heavenly Father feeds them. Are you not much more valuable than they? Can any one of you by worrying add a single hour to your life?

Next 7 Days
on your Faith Journey
with Abba

For these 7 days reflect on the scriptures then add what you are seeing and hearing. Write down where the verse takes you spiritually.

Tracking Faith with Abba

Keep track of your journey as you go.

Day 1	
Day 2	
Day 3	
Day 4	
Day 5	
Day 6	
Day 7	

Day 29) Habakkuk 3:19

The Sovereign Lord is my strength;
he makes my feet like the feet of a deer,
he enables me to tread on the heights.

Day 30) Romans 8:28

And we know that in all things God works for the good of those who love him, who have been called according to his purpose.

Day 31) Deuteronomy 2:7

The Lord your God has blessed you in all the work of your hands. He has watched over your journey through this vast wilderness. These forty years the Lord your God has been with you, and you have not lacked anything.

Day 32) 1 Corinthians 13:4-7

Love is patient, love is kind. It does not envy, it does not boast, it is not proud. It does not dishonor others, it is not self-seeking, it is not easily angered, it keeps no record of wrongs. Love does not delight in evil but rejoices with the truth. It always protects, always trusts, always hopes, always perseveres.

Day 33) Proverbs 37:4-6

for the Lord will be at your side
and will keep your foot from being snared.

Day 34) Proverbs 3:26

Take delight in the Lord,
and he will give you the desires of your heart. Commit your way to the Lord;
trust in him and he will do this: He will make your righteous reward shine like
the dawn, your vindication like the noonday sun.

Day 35) Luke 6:38

Give, and it will be given to you. A good measure, pressed down, shaken together and running over, will be poured into your lap. For with the measure you use, it will be measured to you."

Next 14 Days
on your Faith Journey
with Abba

Reflection week of how you view yourself in the scriptures.

Write down where the verse takes you spiritually.

Tracking Faith with Abba

Keep track of your journey as you go.

Day 1	
Day 2	
Day 3	
Day 4	
Day 5	
Day 6	
Day 7	
Day 8	
Day 9	
Day 10	
Day 11	
Day 12	
Day 13	
Day 14	

Day 36) John 7:38

Whoever believes in me, as Scripture has said, rivers of living water will flow from within them

Day 37) Exodus 15:2

"The Lord is my strength and my defense
      he has become my salvation.
He is my God, and I will praise him,
      my father's God, and I will exalt him

Day 38) Deuteronomy 31:6

Be strong and courageous. Do not be afraid or terrified because of them, for the Lord your God goes with you; he will never leave you nor forsake you."

Day 39) Romans 5:8

But God demonstrates his own love for us in this: While we were still sinners, Christ died for us

Day 40) Psalm 23:1-3

The Lord is my shepherd, 1 lack nothing. He makes me lie down in green pastures, he leads me beside quiet waters, he refreshes my soul.
He guides me along the right paths for his name's sake.

Day 41) Romans 8:14

For those who are led by the Spirit of God are the children of God

Day 42) Habakkuk 2:2

Then the Lord replied: "Write down the revelation
    and make it plain on tablets
    so that a herald may run with it.

Day 43) Habakkuk 2:3

For the revelation awaits an appointed time;
    it speaks of the end
    and will not prove false.
Though it linger, wait for it;
    it will certainly come
    and will not delay

Day 44) Psalms 16:11

You make known to me the path of life;
    you will fill me with joy in your presence,
    with eternal pleasures at your right hand

Day 45) Philippians 4:13

I can do all this through him who gives me strength

Day 46) John 1:51

He then added, "Very truly I tell you, you will see 'heaven open, and the angels of God ascending and descending on the Son of Man."

Day 47) James 1:5-6

If any of you lacks wisdom, you should ask God, who gives generously to all without finding fault, and it will be given to you. But when you ask, you must believe and not doubt, because the one who doubts is like a wave of the sea, blown and tossed by the wind.

Day 48) Isaiah 40:31

but those who hope in the Lord
     will renew their strength.
They will soar on wings like eagles;
     they will run and not grow weary,
     they will walk and not be faint.

Day 49) Philippians 4:7

And the peace of God, which transcends all understanding, will guard your hearts and your minds in Christ Jesus.

Next 14 Days
on your Faith Journey
with Abba

Reflect!! Reflect!!

Now write down how you would like to see yourself in these

scriptures.

Tracking Faith with Abba

Keep track of your journey as you go.

Day 1	
Day 2	
Day 3	
Day 4	
Day 5	
Day 6	
Day 7	
Day 8	
Day 9	
Day 10	
Day 11	
Day 12	
Day 13	
Day 14	

Day 50) Psalms 27:1

The Lord is my light and my salvation—
    whom shall I fear?
The LORD is the stronghold of my life—
      of whom shall I be afraid?

Day 51) Galatians 6:9

Let us not become weary in doing good, for at the proper time we will reap a harvest if we do not give up.

Day 52) Ephesians 4:2

Be completely humble and gentle; be patient, bearing with one another in love.

Day 53) John 14:26-27

But the Advocate, the Holy Spirit, whom the Father will send in my name, will teach you all things and will remind you of everything I have said to you. Peace I leave with you; my peace I give you. I do not give to you as the world gives. Do not let your hearts be troubled and do not be afraid.

Day 54) Psalms 116:1-2

I love the LORD, for he heard my voice; he heard my cry for mercy. Because he turned his ear to me, I will call on him as long as I live.

Day 55) Romans 8:14

For those who are led by the Spirit of God are the children of God.

Day 56) Isaiah 30:21

Whether you turn to the right or to the left, your ears will hear a voice behind you, saying, "This is the way; walk in it."

Day 57) Psalms 121:1-2

I lift up my eyes to the mountains—
> where does my help come from? My help comes from the LORD, the Maker of heaven and earth.

Day 58) Matthew 11:28

"Come to me, all you who are weary and burdened, and I will give you rest.

Day 59) Deuteronomy 8:18

But remember the Lord your God, for it is he who gives you the ability to produce wealth, and so confirms his covenant, which he swore to your ancestors, as it is today

Day 60) 1 Peter 5:10

And the God of all grace, who called you to his eternal glory in Christ, after you have suffered a little while, will himself restore you and make you strong, firm and steadfast.

Day 61) Isaiah 40:29

He gives strength to the weary
    and increases the power of the weak.

Day 62) 2 Corinthians 12:9-10

But he said to me, "My grace is sufficient for you, for my power is made perfect in weakness." Therefore, I will boast all the more gladly about my weaknesses, so that Christ's power may rest on me. That is why, for Christ's sake, I delight in weaknesses, in insults, in hardships, in persecutions, in difficulties. For when I am weak, then I am strong.

Day 63) Psalms 31:24

Be strong and take heart,
     all you who hope in the Lord.

Next 14 Days
on your Faith Journey
with Abba

Reflect!! Reflect!! Reflect!!

Now combine what you're hearing, seeing, and feeling when

you read these scriptures. Write down where the verses take you

spiritually.

Tracking Faith with Abba

Keep track of your journey as you go.

Day 1	
Day 2	
Day 3	
Day 4	
Day 5	
Day 6	
Day 7	
Day 8	
Day 9	
Day 10	
Day 11	
Day 12	
Day 13	
Day 14	

Day 64) Isaiah 12:2

Surely God is my salvation;
I will trust and not be afraid.
The Lord, the Lord himself, is my strength and my defense;
he has become my salvation."

Day 65) 1 Corinthians 15:58

Therefore, my dear brothers and sisters, stand firm. Let nothing move you. Always give yourselves fully to the work of the Lord, because you know that your labor in the Lord is not in vain.

Day 66) Jeremiah 29:11

For I know the plans I have for you," declares the Lord, "plans to prosper you and not to harm you, plans to give you hope and a future.

Day 67) Lamentations 3:22-23

Because of the Lord's great love we are not consumed,
for his compassions never fail.
They are new every morning;
great is your faithfulness.

Day 68) 1 John 4:18

There is no fear in love. But perfect love drives out fear, because fear has to do with punishment. The one who fears is not made perfect in love.

Day 69) 1 Peter 3:14

But even if you should suffer for what is right, you are blessed. "Do not fear their threats; do not be frightened."

Day 70) 2 Corinthians 5:7

For we live by faith, not by sight.

Day 71) Psalms 32:8

I will instruct you and teach you in the way you should go;
I will counsel you with my loving eye on you.

Day 72) James 3:18

Peacemakers who sow in peace reap a harvest of righteousness.

Day 73) John 8:32

Then you will know the truth, and the truth will set you free."

Day 74) 2 Timothy 1:7

For the Spirit God gave us does not make us timid, but gives us power, love and self-discipline.

Day 75) Proverbs 1:2

for gaining wisdom and instruction;
for understanding words of insight;

Day 76) Isaiah 26:3

You will keep in perfect peace
those whose minds are steadfast,
because they trust in you.

Day 77) Psalms 119:76

May your unfailing love be my comfort,
according to your promise to your servant.

Next 14 Days
on your Faith Journey
with Abba

Reflect!! Reflect!! Reflect!!

Now combine what you're hearing, seeing, and feeling when

you read these scriptures. Write down where the verses take you

spiritually.

Tracking Faith with Abba

Keep track of your journey as you go.

Day 1	
Day 2	
Day 3	
Day 4	
Day 5	
Day 6	
Day 7	
Day 8	
Day 9	
Day 10	
Day 11	
Day 12	
Day 13	
Day 14	

Day 78) 1 Corinthians 16:14

Do everything in love.

Day 79) 1 John 4:8

Whoever does not love does not know God, because God is love.

Day 80) Deuteronomy 31:6

Be strong and courageous. Do not be afraid or terrified because of them, for the Lord your God goes with you; he will never leave you nor forsake you."

Day 81) Psalms 29:11

The Lord gives strength to his people;
    the LORD blesses his people with peace.

Day 82) Proverbs 3:13-15

Blessed are those who find wisdom,
> those who gain understanding, for she is more profitable than silver
> and yields better returns than gold. She is more precious than rubies;
> nothing you desire can compare with her.

Day 83) Psalms 118:24

The Lord has done it this very day;
> let us rejoice today and be glad.

Day 84) Isaiah 61:10

I delight greatly in the LORD;
    my soul rejoices in my God.
For he has clothed me with garments of salvation
    and arrayed me in a robe of his righteousness,
as a bridegroom adorns his head like a priest,
    and as a bride adorns herself with her jewels.

Day 85) Proverbs 19:20

Listen to advice and accept discipline,
    and at the end you will be counted among the wise.

Day 86) John 3:16

For God so loved the world that he gave his one and only Son, that whoever believes in him shall not perish but have eternal life.

Day 87) Psalms 138:8

The LORD will vindicate me;
    your love, Lord, endures forever—
    do not abandon the works of your hands.

Day 88) Psalms 42:7

Deep calls to deep
     in the roar of your waterfalls;
all your waves and breakers
     have swept over me.

Day 89) Jeremiah 31:3

The Lord appeared to us in the past, saying:
     "I have loved you with an everlasting love;
     I have drawn you with unfailing kindness.

Day 90) Romans 8:18

I consider that our present sufferings are not worth comparing with the glory that will be revealed in us.

REFLECTION NOTES
Reflect on your spiritual goals to continue to stay on track with Yahweh.

Proverbs 3:5-6
Trust in the LORD with all your heart and lean not on your own understanding; In all your ways submit to him, and he will make your paths straight.

REFLECTION NOTES
Reflect on your spiritual goals to continue to stay on track with Yahweh.

Proverbs 3:5-6
Trust in the LORD with all your heart and lean not on your own understanding; In all your ways submit to him, and he will make your paths straight.

REFLECTION NOTES
Reflect on your spiritual goals to continue to stay on track with Yahweh.

Proverbs 3:5-6
Trust in the LORD with all your heart and lean not on your own understanding; In all your ways submit to him, and he will make your paths straight.